Terraria

Tips, Hints, Cheats, Strategy And Walkthrough

DISCLAIMER

Maple Tree Books

If you want to get access to upcoming books on various topics, 'like' our Facebook page to be informed. We always offer the books for free for 5 days when they are first released. You can download them when they are free and benefit from them :)

Go to this website and enter your name and email to join our mailing list.

https://www.Facebook.com/mapletreebooks

And oh, dont forget to leave a review :)

Even if you did not benefit from this book at all we still want to hear from your feedback so we can improve in the future :)

Alternatively you can join our mailing list

http://www.MapleTreeBooks.com

You can join our Twitter page as well

https://Twitter.com/MapleTreeBooks1

Thanks for reading :)

We wish you success in this life and in the next.

What Will You Find In This Guide?

Developed by Re-Logic Game Studio, Terraria is an action packed adventurous game, officially launched on May, 16, 2011. Fight, Dig, Build, Explore! Your options in this game are limitless.

'Terraria' is an extremely addictive game that will keep you hooked literally for hours. The game is often compared to the popular sandbox building game 'Minecraft'. Your imagination and creativity is highly rewarded when you play this exciting game.

From making weapons to digging deep underground to uncover hidden accessories, money and other valuables, from fighting tough enemies and monsters in a number of biomes, to gathering stone, ores, wood and other resources to build and defend your **Terraria** world, the game has something for everyone.

You will be provided with a limited number of resources in this game and you are required to utilize them in the best possible manner to defend yourself against the nocturnal monsters.

If you are really excited to play **'Terraria'** but have no clue about how you can survive, you have come to the right place. This beginner's guide includes the best tips, hints, cheats, hacks and strategy to help you get the highest scores in your favorite game.

In short, you get to know everything that'll help you become a master of this adventurous and fun packed game. Continue reading to "walk through" the highly addictive game known as **'Terraria'**.

So what are you waiting for?! Grab your tools and get ready to face the challenge. Can you dig it?!

TABLE OF CONTENTS

Chapter 1

Terraria-An Introduction for the Newbies

Officially launched on May 16, 2011, 'Terraria' is an action packed adventurous game developed by Re-Logic game studio. Imagination and creativity are the attributes required for playing this game.

From making your own weapons to digging deep underground to reveal accessories, money and other valuables that are hidden in the ground, from fighting monsters and tough enemies in a variety of different biomes or environments to collecting ores, stones, wood and other resources to build and defend your Terraria world, the game has something for everyone.

Players will be provided with a limited number of resources in this game and they are required to utilize them in the best possible manner to defend themselves against the nocturnal monsters and tough enemies.

The game invites players to explore and dig for getting building materials at the same time spawning big monsters off screen. As soon as the player starts the game, he is challenged to come up with intelligent solutions to protecting themselves from monsters utilizing the available sources in the most effective manner. Players will be provided with a number of weapons, armor and equipment, to defend themselves against strong enemies and bosses.

Based on the size of the world selected by the player, the worlds in Terraria are randomly generated. The game features a number of different biomes/environments including, *Forests, Jungle, Snow Biome, Deserts, Underground, Cavern, Underground Jungle, the Corruption, The Underworld, Floating Islands* and *Dungeon*.

Each zone featured on this game revolves around a precise theme and showcases a specific set of treasures, ores, plants and monsters.

Furthermore, players will be facing a number of dangerous monsters during the game play including, *Angry Bones, Giant worm, Antlion, Goblin Scout, Bald Zombie, Goldfish, Bat,*

Harpy, Bird, Homet, Blazing wheel, Jellyfish, Bone Serpent, Man Eater, Bunny, Meteor Head, Corrupt Bunny, Piranha, Corrupt Goldfish, Servant of Cthulhu, Crab, Shark, Cursed Skull, Skeleton, Dark Caster, Slime, Demon, Snatcher, Demon eye, Spike ball, Devourer, Voodoo Demon, Vulture and *Dungeon Guardian*. In order to proceed to the next level players will be required to beat these monsters in deadly fights.

These monsters are further augmented by bosses. These bosses can be summoned for fight under given conditions.

Often compared to the popular sandbox building game 'Minecraft', the main purpose of Terraria is to give players a classic experience of exploring, digging, crafting, mining, fighting, sculpting and building your own world-all in a single game. Exciting-isn't it!

Chapter 2
Exploring the Game and Understanding the Basics

Get to Know the Different Game modes

Players will be asked to select a game mode in the opening screen of the game play. The two games modes offered on Terraria include Single Player mode or Multiplayer mode.

If you are playing for the first time, it is recommended to select Single Player mode. It is very easy to learn when playing in Single Player mode.

Getting Started

Creating your Character

To enhance the gaming experience while playing the game, Terraria allows players to create their own character through a character creation screen that showcases different character properties such as hair, eyes, skin and clothes.

Players can choose their customized settings from a list of options for each of the character properties mentioned above. In addition to cosmetic changes, players can also change the gender of their character. Nonetheless, if you want to keep the default settings, you can skip the process.

Create your Terraria World

Once you are done with character creation, you will be presented with three world size options including small, medium and large.

It you are playing it for the first time, it is recommended for you to select the small world size as it is going to make it easier for you to explore and experience the thrilling Terraria world. Once you are familiar with the small world, you can choose medium and large size worlds for bigger and greater exposure.

Dig it, Build it, and defend it!-The Game Interface

You character will usually be placed in the centre of a Forest when you first enter the Terraria world. This default location is called spawn point. As your character is centrally placed, you can explore the Terraria world in the right and the left directions.

- **Inventory Slots**

You will notice ten boxes in the upper left corner of your screen numbered from 1-0. These are inventory slots called the 'hotbar' contain items players currently have access to. When you begin your game, you will usually find a Copper Axe-used to chop down trees to get wood, a Copper Pickaxe-used to dig up stone and dirt and a Copper Shortsword- used for fighting enemies.

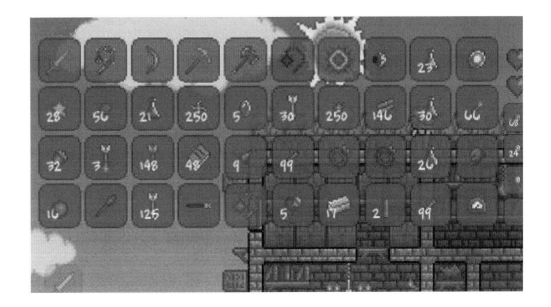

S. No	Inventory	Slots	Description
1.	Hot Bar	20 Slots	Current Useable Items Appear in the hot bar
2.	Storage	30 Slots	Any item can be placed/stored here
3.	Coins	4 Slots	The slot contains picked up coins or coins acquired by selling items
4.	Ammo	4 Slots	These slots are used for storing ammunition
5.	Trash Can	1 Slot	These slots are used for discarding items
6.	Clothing	3 Slots	These slots are used for Armor
7.	Social	3 Slots	Armor, Vanity items and other items can be placed in these slots
8.	Storage Items Inventory	20 Slots	New items can be found and excess items can be stored in these slots
9.	NPC Inventory	20 Slots	Items available for purchase are displayed in these slots

- **Health Points**

At the top of your screen, you will notice hearts. These hearts indicate the health of the character. Each heart represents 20 health points. When you begin the game, you have 5 hearts or 100 health points. Players can increase their health points to 400 represented by 20 hearts using life crystals. It is essential for you to know that both players and monsters have health points.

Health points can be decreased when players take damage from drowning, environmental hazards such as touching lava, meteorite and hell stone or through fall damage. The heart slowly fades away as the damage is taken and when a character's life reaches zero, death occurs.

Nonetheless, there are a number of items that can be used to restore health including, *heart* (restores 20 health points), *mushrooms* (restores 15 health points), *lesser healing potion* (restores 50 health points), *glowing mushroom* (restores 25 health points), *healing potion* (restores 100 health points), *greater healing potion* (restores 150 health points), *restoration potion* (restores 100 mana and 100 health points), *Goldfish* (restores 20 health points), *lesser restoration potion* (restores 50 mana and 50 health points), *life crystal* (restores 20 health points and increases maximum health points by 20), *Band of regeneration* (slowly restores health when it is worn), *band of regeneration* (restores 60 health points) and *bottled water* (restores 20 health points).

- Mana

Mana is a resource that can be used by players when using magical items and weapons. When you begin your game you will be starting with zero Mana. Players can increase their Mana using

Mana crystals that are crafted from fallen stars). They are represented by a vertical meter of blue stars that appears on the right side of your screen.

Mana can be restored using a number of items including, *lesser Mana Potion* (restores 50 Mana), *Mana Potion* (restores 100 Mana), *Greater Mana Potion* (Restores 200 Mana), *lesser restoration Potion* (restores 50 Mana), *Restoration Potion* (restores 100 Mana), Stars (restores 100 Mana), *Mana Crystal* (restores 20 Mana and increases 20 Mana), *Mana regeneration Potion* (increase Mana regeneration).

Additionally, there are a number of items that can be used to increase Mana such as, *Band of Starpower* (increases Mana by 1 star), *Jungle hat* (increases Mana by 1 star), *Jungle shirt* (increases Mana by 1 star), *Cobalt hat* (increases Mana by 2 stars), *Mythril Hood* (increases Mana by 3 stars), *Adamantite headgear* (increases Mana by 4 stars), *Hallowed Headgear* (increases Mana by 5 stars) and *Crystal ball* (increases Mana by 1 star).

- **Common Enemies**

Players will encounter a number of common enemies during the game play including,

Angry Bones, Giant worm, Antlion, Goblin Scout, Bald Zombie, Goldfish, Bat, Harpy, Bird, Homet, Blazing wheel, Jellyfish, Bone Serpent, Man Eater, Bunny, Meteor Head, Corrupt

Bunny, Piranha, Corrupt Goldfish, Servant of Cthulhu, Crab, Shark, Cursed Skull, Skeleton, Dark Caster, Slime, Demon, Snatcher, Demon eye, Spike ball, Devourer, Voodoo Demon, Vulture and *Dungeon Guardian.*

- **Bosses**

The enemies in the Terraria world are augmented by some dangerous and creepy monsters including, *Wall of Flesh, Skeletron, Eater of Worlds, King Slime* and *Eye of Cthulhu.*

- **Items**

Players will be able to find a number of items on the Terraria world to survive and combat with monsters. These items include *Tools, Weapons, Furniture, Soils, Blocks, Accessories, and Gems, Defense items, Vanity items, Statues, Potions* and other *miscellaneous items.*

- **Crafting Stations**

When in Terraria world, players can craft a number of items within the range of their crafting stations (pieces of furniture required to craft various items). There are eighteen crafting stations featured in the game. These include,

Adamantite Forge, Alchemy Station, Bookcase, Furnace, Cooking pot, Demon Altar, Hellforge, Keg, Loom, Sawmill, Tinkerer's Workshop, Mythril Anvil, Iron Anvil, Wooden Chair, Wooden Table and Work Bench.

- **NPC**

In the Terraria world, you will be able to find NPC's or the Non player characters that provide some service to players. A number of NPC's are vendors selling items in exchange for coins. Other NPC's featured on the game include the *Guide* that provides information, the *Nurse* that offers Health restoration and the *Oldman* that summons the Skeletron.

The NPC's featured on the game include the *Arms dealer, Demolitionist, Dryad, Goblin Tinkerer, Mechanic, Nurse, Santa Claus, Wizard, Old man*, *Clothier* and *Merchant.*

Chapter 3
Walkthrough

Featured Environments/Biomes

You will find a wide variety of environments in the Terraria world called Biomes. Each environment/biome is based on a specific theme featuring engaging graphics and sound play that overall enhances the ambiance of the game play.

EXPLORING THE SURFACE

1. THE FOREST BIOME

The forest Biome is primarily composed of trees and dirt stones. It is perhaps the easiest environment well suited for beginners. The monsters/enemies featured in this environment are also the weakest in comparison to other biomes.

The monsters featured on this Biome include, *Blue Slime*, *Purple Slime*, *Green Slime* and *Pinky*. The monster drops *gel* and *Day bloom*; *Mushroom*, *Iron* and *Copper* are the prominent resources available on the forest biome. The chest contents (storage items) available on this biome include *Blowpipe, Spear, Wooden Boomerang*, *Bottle* and *Throwing knife*. The recommended life for Forest Biome is 5 hearts.

Building a Shelter

Building a shelter is the foremost thing to do when starting a new world. It is significant to begin by collecting/gathering building materials such as stone or wood. Furthermore, it is essential to explore the immediate area before the sun goes down. You will be able to find iron in the area nearby that can be utilized to get an early Anvil (used to craft weapons, armor and tools). It is advisable to return to your shelter before it is dark.

When the Night Falls

Players are advised to stay in their shelters during the night especially if they are beginners. The monsters/enemies coming out at night can be difficult to deal with. These monsters can be killed to make money.

Furthermore, players can make mine in a cave during the night. It is essential for you to know that some monsters will make their way into the cave, but it is not very difficult to deal with them.

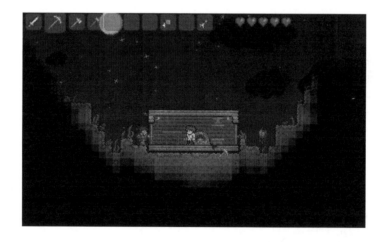

Moreover, during night time an event called Blood Moon will occur after you have spent a little while on the game. When 'BloodMoon' occurs, the spawn rate of monsters temporarily increases. If you are a beginner, it is recommended to stay indoors. Monsters you may come across during night include, ***Zombie***, ***Demon Eye***, ***The Groom*** and ***Corrupt Bunny*** (appearing only during BloodMoon).

Building a base

After building your temporary shelter, it is time for you to start working on building a base. Players can organize inventories and craft weapons in these bases. It may take a little long to create a fully fledged base, but it is suggested to take your time when building bases.

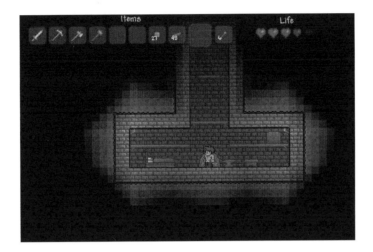

Exploring/Discovering the Surface

The surface is rich with different ores of copper and iron deposits. It is essential for you to look for these ores in order to craft/build armor and new tools before you can begin with the mining process. Furthermore, you will be able to find chests (storage item that is used for storing other items) at the entrance of some caves.

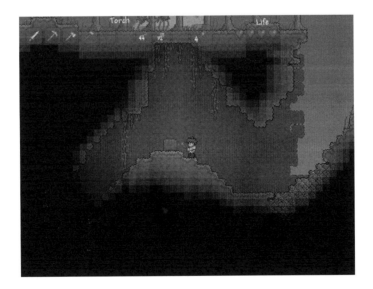

EXPLORING THE UNDERGROUND

Once you have explored the surface, it is time to begin the mining process. There are a number of methods you can use for mining such as digging a shaft, cave hopping etc. Each of these methods have its own merits and demerits.

If you are digging a shaft, it will allow you to gain access to deeper mine areas. Exploring and digging caves that spawn naturally is another popular technique of mining. When you approach a dead end in the cave, you can use your tools and torch lights to find other caves. This technique is referred to as cave hopping. Players can use a combination of techniques that best suits their existing needs.

2. THE UNDERGROUND BIOME

Underground is the first layer that you will find below the surface. The monsters featured on this biome/environment include, **Red Slime**, **Yellow Slime**, **Blue Slime**, **Blue**, **Pinky**, **Jellyfish** and **Giant Worm**. These monsters drop **Whoopie cushion**, **Glowstick** and **Gel. Binkroot**.

Glowing Mushroom, **Gems**, **Silver**, **Iron** and **copper** are the most prominent resources available on the Underground Biome. The chest contents or storage items featured on this biome include, **Magic mirror**, **Angel Statue**, **Band of Regeneration**, **Hermes Boots**, **Cloud in a bottle**, **Jester's arrow** and **Enchanted Boomerang**. The recommended life for this biome is 5 hearts.

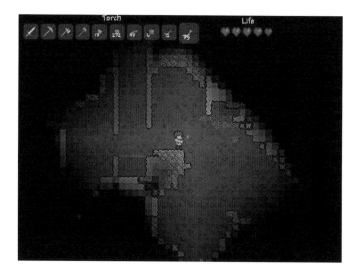

When in this Biome, it is advised to find iron and copper. Before proceeding to the next layer, players are suggested to obtain silver weapons and full iron armor. You should also try to get at least two to three life crystals to improve your health points.

3. THE CAVERN BIOME

Beneath the Underground layer is the Cavern layer. This layer is particularly rich in gems and mineral deposits. The monsters featured on this biome include, *Tim, Mother Slime, Baby Slime, Black Slime, Giant Worm, Skeleton, Blue Jellyfish, Tim, Undead Miner, Piranha, Pinky* and *Cave bat*. These monsters drop, *Whoopie cushion, Hook, Gel, Wizard hat* and *Robot hat. Copper,*

Iron, Gold, Silver, Gems, Demonite, Lava and *Blinkroot* are the chest contents or the storage items featured on this biome. The recommended life for this biome is 8 hearts.

Players should focus on obtaining Silver equipment and Gold Equipment when in Cavern Biome. Furthermore, it is essential for players to look for at least 3-4 life crystals when in this layer. This layer may be a little dangerous for beginners.

Unless you have obtained Iron equipment, players should not make an attempt to progress through Cavern Biome. It is also recommended to bring potions when entering this layer/environment.

It is recommended not to mine too deep in this layer as it may result in spawning monsters of the Underworld layer. These monsters are not easy to deal with even if you are a medium level player.

<h2 style="text-align:center">REVISITING THE SURFACE</h2>

A number of mid-tier biomes will open up, once you manage to obtain the complete Gold Equipment. These biomes are rich in Alchemy ingredients and other treasures. At this stage it is recommended to have at least ten NPC houses therefore, it there are any NPC houses that have been not built as yet you should complete building it.

4. THE DESERT BIOME

As the name suggests, the Desert Biome is a sandy biome/environment. *Antlion*, *Vulture* and *Mummy* are the monsters featured on the desert biome. These monsters drop *Antlion Mandible* and Light and Dark *Shard*.

Cactus and Waterleaf are the notable resources available, whereas; the recommended equipment for this biome is Iron equipment. The monsters spawning in this layer are not very difficult to deal with. The recommended heart life for this layer is 7 hearts.

5. THE JUNGLE BIOME

The Jungle biome is primarily composed of Jungle trees, Mud, Vines and Grass against a dark green background. The monsters featured on this biome include, *Snatcher*, *Piranha*, *Doctor Bones* (spawns during the night), *Jungle Bat* and *Jungle Slime*.

The loot items dropped by these monsters include *Archaeologist's Hat*, *Hook*, *Gel* and *Robot Hat*. *Jungle Spores*, *Jungle Rose* and *Moonglow* are the notable resources available on the jungle biome. The recommended life for playing this biome is 10 hearts. Desert is one of the most difficult biomes and it is recommended to obtain *Gold Equipment* before attempting to explore this biome.

6. THE CORRUPTION BIOME

The Corruption biome mainly consists of Grass and Tress against a Purple Background. The monsters featured on this biome include, *Eater of Souls*, *Little Eater*, *Big Eater*, *Piranha* and *Corrupt Goldfish*. The monsters drop *Rotten Chunk*, *Hook*, *Robot Hat* and *Worm Tooth*.

Deathweed, *Demonite* and *Wild Mushrooms* are the notable resources on this biome. *Gold* is the recommended equipment on this biome and the recommended life for playing the Corruption biome is 10 hearts.

It is worthwhile to mention that Corruption is a very difficult surface biome especially due to the flying enemy Eater of Souls. The biome features **Shadow Orbs** (purple floating spheres that can be found in the chasms (deep tunnels) of the biome.

Smashing shadow orbs can help you obtain powerful items such as **Band of Starpower, Musket, Ball O'Hurt, Orb of light** and **Vilethorn**. You need to be careful when smashing these Orbs as it results in swarming of **Eater of Worlds** and if you are not careful these flying enemies can damage your health points.

7. THE OCEAN BIOME

Below the surface of each biome/map, you will find the Ocean Biome. The enemies featured on this biome include, **Crab, Jellyfish, Pink** and **Shark**. These enemies drop loot items including **Diving Helmet, Shark fin** and **GlowStick** when you kill them. Coral is the most notable resource showcased on this biome. The chest contents featured on this biome include **Trident, Flipper** and **Breathing Reed**.

The recommended equipment when exploring the Ocean biome is **Gills Potions** and **Gold** equipment, whereas the recommended life is 10 hearts. The Ocean is known for its **Chest contents** and **Alchemy ingredients**. The biome is not an easy one to explore and beginners may have breathing issues without Alchemy ingredients such as Waterleaf.

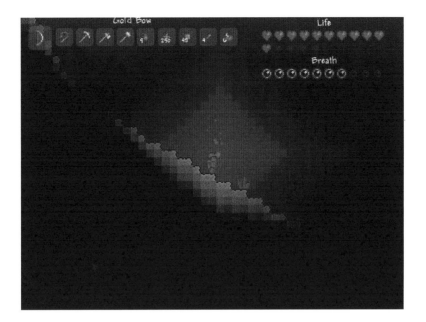

8. THE SNOW BIOME

Between 15 and 31st December, the snow biomes are generated in all environments covering everything such as Trees, Dirt and Grass with snow. The monsters featured on Snow Biome include *Purple Slime*, *Green Slime*, *Blue Slime* and *Pinky*. These monsters drop *Gel* when they are killed, whereas *snow blocks* are the most notable resource available on this biome.

SUMMONING THE EYE OF CTHULHU

If you have successfully managed to have 10 or more hearts or you have not defeated Eye of Cthulhu in the current biome or four NPC's (Non Player Characters) have moved into houses in the present world Eye of Cthulhu has a good chance of spawning every night.

The recommended equipment to fight with this tough enemy includes **Ranged Weapons**, **Hunter Potions**, **Ironskin Potions**, **Gold** and **Regeneration Potions** whereas a player should have at least 10 hearts when summoning Eye of Cthulhu. The loot items dropped by the boss include **Corrupt Seeds**, **Demonite Ores** and **Unholy Arrows**. Ranged weapons including **Bow**, **Shuriken** are the most effective weapons that can be used against Eye of Cthulhu.

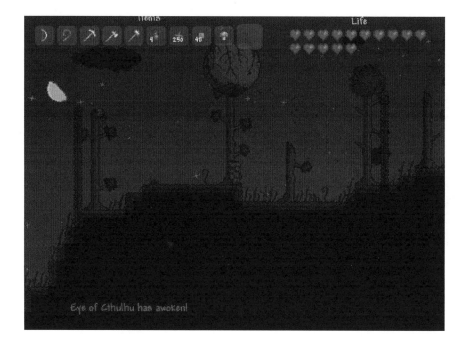

SUMMONING THE EATER OF WORLDS

Once you have defeated the Eye of Cthulhu you will have to fight the **Eater of Worlds.** Every time a player smashes Shadow orbs for the third time, Eater of Worlds will spawn. Nonetheless, using Shadow Orbs drops such as Ball O' Hurt and Vilethorn can help players defeat this tough enemy.

The loot items dropped by the Boss include Shadow Scale and Demonite ores. Gold, Ironskin Potions, Piercing Weapons and Hunter Potions is the recommended equipment that can be used to defeat the enemy whereas a player should have at least 12 hearts to fight the boss. It is worthwhile to mention that players need to fight the Eater of World in the Corruption biome.

9. THE METEORITE BIOME

Whenever a Meteorite crashes into a site, it results in leaving a crater that is filled with meteorite ore. The event can occur in any biome/environment. Players will be notified upon the occurrence of the event.

Meteor Head is the only monster featured on this biome/environment. The biome is rich in meteorite resource. Dynamite, Obsidian Skull and Shadow is the recommended equipment for this biome, whereas a player should have at least 12 hearts when exploring the meteorite biome.

It is worthwhile to mention that meteorite blocks can damage your health. Therefore, it is recommended to equip with Obsidian Skull to prevent the damage due to Meteorite blocks.

SUMMONING THE SKELETRON

After you have obtained the meteor equipment and the shadow equipment, players can explore the dungeon biome. But before exploring the dungeon biome/environment, you need to defeat the Skeleton. In order to summon the Skeleton, players need to have a talk with the Oldman that can be found at night in front of the Dungeon.

Meteor, Shadow, Piercing Weapons and Ironskin Potions are the recommended equipments that can be used efficiently against the boss, whereas the recommended health life is 15 hearts. After defeating the Skeleton, players can now explore the Dungeon biome/environment.

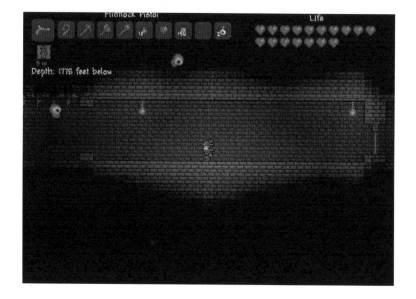

10. THE DUNGEON BIOME

The Dungeon biome is a vast biome lined with bricks. The monsters featured on this biome include *Big Boned, Short Bones, Blazing Wheel, Angry Bones, Dark Caster, Dungeon Slime* and *Spike Ball* and *Cursed Skull*. The monster drops loot items such as *Gold key* and *Bone*.

Water Bolt, Life crystal, Chain Lantern and *Switch* are the most notable resources available on this biome. The chest contents featured on this biome include *Blue Scepter, Cobalt, Shield, Blue Moon, Magic, Missile, Muramasa* and *Shadow key*. *Meteor* and *Shadow* is the recommended equipment and the recommended health life for playing this biome is 15 hearts.

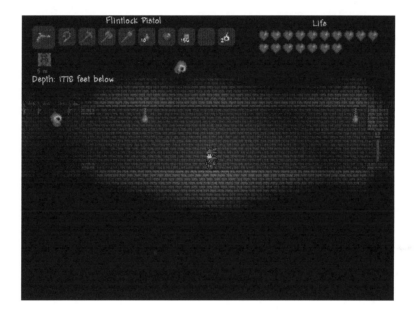

The dungeon biome contains a wealth of treasures such as *Water Bolts* and *Life crystals*. It is recommended to collect as much treasure as you can as it can be very useful as you progress through the game play. Furthermore, it is essential to keep the golden keys obtained in the biome, as these keys (at least three of them) are required to open the chests in the Floating Island biome.

11. THE FLOATING ISLAND BIOME

Floating Island is a piece of Forest land floating in the sky, hence the name. The monster featured on this biome is called *Harpy* and it drops feather. *Silver* and *gold* are the most notable resources found on this biome, whereas **Shiny Red Balloon, Starfury, Lucky Horseshoe** are the chest contents found on the Floating island.

Gravitation Potions and **Gold** are the recommended equipment for exploring this biome and players should have at least 10 hearts to play this game.

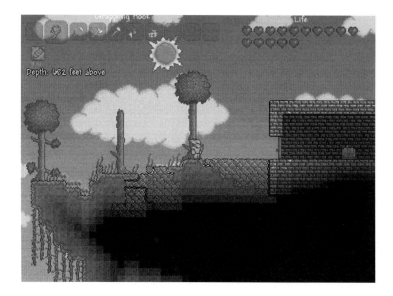

Using the golden keys obtained in the Dungeon biome, players will be able to unlock the treasure chests found on the Floating island. You can choose to explore the Biome anytime during the game play using **Gravitation Potions**.

12. THE UNDERGROUND JUNGLE BIOME

After you have explored the Jungle biome, you can now explore the next biome called the Underground Jungle. The Underground Jungle lies below the Jungle surface and if you mine deeply, you should be able to enter yet another biome featured on this thrilling game.

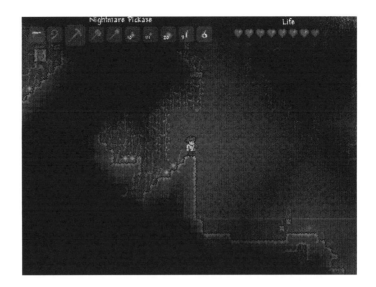

The monsters featured on this biome include Dragon Stinger, Piranha, Jungle Bat, Big Stinger, Hornet and Little Stinger. The loot items dropped by monsters include Hook, Robot Hat and Stinger.

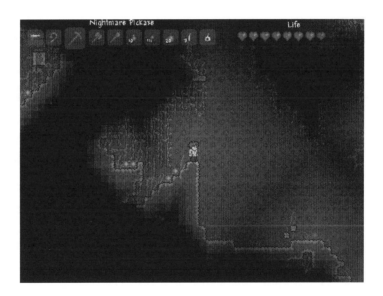

The notable resources available on this biome include ***Jungle Rose, Nature's Gift, Jungle Spores*** and ***Moonglow***. ***Staff of Re growth***, ***Anklet of the wind*** and ***Feral Claws*** are the chest contents featured on the Underground Jungle Biome. The recommended equipments when exploring this biome include, ***Dungeon weapons***, ***Necro***, ***Meteor*** and ***Shadow,*** whereas players should have at least 15 hearts when playing this level.

It is worthwhile to mention that the Underground Jungle Biome is one of the most difficult biomes featuring tough enemies. It is probably the second most difficult level in the normal mode.

13. THE UNDERWORLD BIOME

The Underworld Biome is perhaps the deepest layer of the Terraria world. Popularly called as Hell, the level can be reached by mining deeply in the Cavern Biome.

The monsters showcased on this biome include *Fire Imp, Demon, Voodoo Demon, Bone Serpent, Hell Bat* and *Lava Slime*. The loot items dropped by monsters include *Guide Voodoo Doll, Demon Scythe* and *Plumber's hat*. The most notable resources available on this biome include *Fireblossom, Hellforge, Demon Torch* and *Hellstone.*

The chests contents found on this biome are *Flamelash, Sunfury, Dark Lance* and *Flower of Fire.* The recommended equipments when exploring this level include *Night Owl Potion, Obsidian Skin Potion, Water Walking Potion, Shadow, Jungle, Meteor,* and *Necro,* whereas players should have at least 20 hearts when entering this level.

The Underground biome is a very difficult level. Beware of the lava as it can cause serious damage to your health. Additionally, you should take extra care when mining Hellstone, as it may produce lava that has a tendency of decreasing your health points in no time.

The enemies showcased on this biome are also very difficult to defeat. Fireimps have the ability to shoot past walls, Hell bats are very difficult to hit and other monsters such as Serpents can move through blocks. Special care should be taken when killing Voodoo demons. If the Voodoo dolls (dropped by Voodoo Demons) drops into the lava, it will summon *Wall of Flesh* (boss).

The stage is considered as the most difficult level in the normal mode. When exploring this level, players should try to find Shadow Chests that can be opened using Shadow keys obtained during the Dungeon round.

SUMMONING THE WALL OF FLESH

Before summoning the Wall of Flesh, players are required to obtain maximum health points, maximum Mana, collect Underworld Tier equipment such as *Molten Pickaxe*, *Fiery Greatsword*, *Phoenix Blaster, Sunfury, Flamelash, Demon Scythe, Dark Lance* and *Flamarang*.

Furthermore, it is also essential for players to gather items and accessories such as *Lucky Horse shoe, Band of Starpower, Feral Claws, Magic Mirror, Nature's Gift* and *Ivy Whip*. Players can combine these accessories at the Tinker's workshop.

You will be needing materials including Copper and Iron to summon difficult bosses in the hard mode. Potions such as Ironskin potions and healing potions can prove to be of significance during the hard mode.

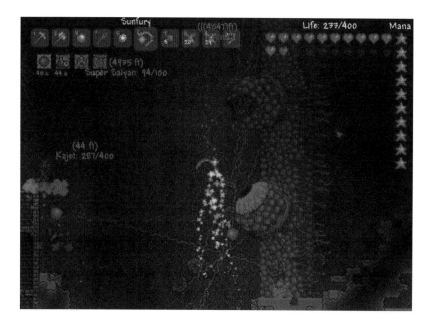

To summon the Wall of Flesh, players need to drop Voodoo dolls dropped by Voodoo Demons into the lava when exploring the Underworld biome. Recommended health life when summoning the Wall of Flesh is 20 hearts. Equipments including ***Jungle, Necro, Shadow, Grappling Hook, Regeneration Potions, Ironskin Potions and Water Walking Potions*** can be used effectively against the ***Wall of Flesh***.

EXPLORING THE TERRARIA WORLD IN HARD MODE

After destroying the ***Wall of Flesh***, the hard mode of the game will be activated. Players will be able to explore the Terraria world in an entirely different manner during the hard mode. The bosses featured in the hard mode are also not easy to deal with.

THE TERRARIA WORLD AT NIGHT (IN HARDMODE)

Extra care should be taken when exploring the Terraria world at night as powerful new monster will spawn at night in the hard mode. The monsters that may emerge at night during the hard mode include ***Wandering Eye, Wraith, Possessed Armor, Clown*** and ***Were Wolf***.

14. THE DESERT BIOME

The monsters featured on the Desert biome (hard mode) include *Antlion, Vulture, Mummy, Dark Mummy* and *Light Mummy*. The loot items dropped by these monsters include Light Shard and Dark Shard, whereas the recommended equipment for playing this biome is *Molten armor*.

15. THE CORRUPTION BIOME

During the hard mode, corruption rapidly spreads by corrupters (attack in packs) that spit an acidic bile that results in spreading corruption. The monsters featured on this biome include

Corrupt Slime, Slimer and Corrupter. *Molten armor* is the recommended equipment when exploring this biome.

16. THE HALLOW BIOME

Hollow spreads rapidly similar to Corruption. Players need to be extra careful when exploring the Biome as the denizens of the Hollow biome are all hostile.

The monsters featured on this biome include *Unicorn, Gastropod* and *Pixie*. The loot drops dropped by these monsters include *Unicorn Horn* and *Pixie Dust*. *Molten Armor* is the recommended equipment when exploring this biome.

Once a player reaches the Corruption level, they should be able to quickly enter the correct chasm. The Chasms/Tunnels of Corruption are comparatively less exposed than the surface showcasing Demon Altars. Systematically destroy Demon Altars. Destroying Demon Altars will result in spawning of Wraiths that may attack the player. Carefully kill these Wraiths before progressing further.

Demon altars spawn ores when destroyed. The first Demon Altar spawns Cobalt ore; the second Demon Altar spawns *Mythril* ore, whereas the third Demon Altar spawns *Adamantite ore*. Before mining new ores, it is essential to destroy as many Demon Altars as possible and collect as much *Cobalt*, *Mythril* and *Adamantite* as you can.

17. THE FLOATING ISLAND BIOME IN HARDMODE

The monsters featured on the Floating Island biome in hard mode include *Wyvern* and *Harpy*. These monsters drop *Feather* and *Soul of Flight* when attacked. The recommended equipment when exploring this biome includes *Gravitation, Ironskin*, *Regeneration Potion* and *Adamantite*. It is worthwhile to mention that you can effectively use piercing equipment against Wyverns.

MINING ORES IN HARD MODE

Once you have spawned enough ores, you should start mining *Adamantite, Mythril* and *Cobalt*. You cannot mine these ores using a normal mode pickaxe. Underground biomes are the most difficult ones found in the hard mode. Before exploring these biomes, players are suggested to bring a good stock of potions such as Regeneration potions, Spelunker potions and Ironskin potions.

18. THE UNDERGROUND BIOME IN HARDMODE

The Underground Biome/Environment is the first layer below the surface. The monsters featured on this biome include *Digger*, *Toxic Sludge* and *Possessed Armor*. Molten Armor and Molten Pickaxe is the recommended equipment when exploring this biome. The layer is not very rich in minerals so it is better to progress through to deeper layers for mining hard mode ores.

19. THE CAVERN BIOME IN HARDMODE

In comparison to the Underground Hallow and the Underground Corruption, the biome is a little less dangerous (mid level difficulty). Due to this mid level difficulty, you can easily mine ores in this level. The monsters featured on this biome include Skeleton *Archer, Giant Bat, Armored Skeleton, Angler Fish* and *Green Jellyfish*. It is recommended to explore this layer with *Molten Armor* and *Molten Pickaxe*.

20. THE UNDERGROUND HALLOW BIOME IN HARDMODE

The Underground Hallow is the second most difficult level in hard mode. The monsters featured on this biome include ***Chaos Elemental***, ***Enchanted Sword***, ***Illuminant Slime*** and ***Illuminant Bat***. The recommended equipment when exploring this layer includes Mythril, Adamantite, Ironskin Potions and Regeneration Potions.

The monsters showcased on this biome drop ***Soul of Light*** (the hardmode crafting material used to craft items such as Crystal Storm, Angel wings etc). ***Crystal Shard*** is the most notable resource found on this biome.

The Underground Corruption is the most difficult biome in the hardmode. The monsters featured on this biome include *World Feeder, Slimer, Devourer, Cursed Hammer, Corrupter, Corrupt Slime* and *Clinger*. These monsters drop Cursed Flame and Soul of Night whereas the recommended equipment when exploring this biome includes *Ironskin Potions, Regeneration Potions, Adamantite* or *Mythril.*

It is essential to obtain Mythril Armor when exploring this biome otherwise it will become very difficult for you to mine ores in this level. Additionally, it is essential for players to upgrade their mining equipments to *Cobalt Drill* as it is going to make mining easier for you.

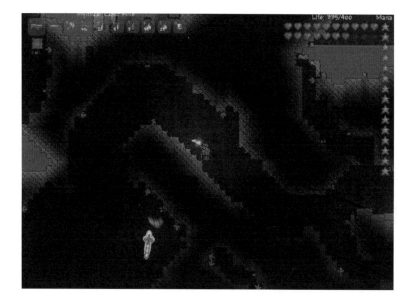

COLLECTING SOULS BEFORE FIGHTING THE HARDMODE BOSSES

It is essential to collect souls and miscellaneous items before fighting the hard mode bosses. Three types of souls are dropped by monsters in the hard mode including *Soul of Light* (that can be collected from monsters in the Underground Hallow), *Soul of Night* (that can be obtained from monsters in the Underground Corruption) and the ***Soul of Flight*** (that can be obtained from monsters in the Floating Island.

THE HARDMODE BOSSES

Hard Mode Boss	Life	Defense
The Destroyer	80,000 health points	Head, Body and Tail
Skeletron Prime	36,000 health points	Head, Canon, Saw, Vice and Laser
The Twins Retinazer Spazmatism	24,000 health points 24,000 health points	First stage and second stage

1. The Destroyer

The Destroyer can be considered as the hard mode version of Eater of Worlds. In comparison to Eater of Worlds it is much longer and moves way faster.

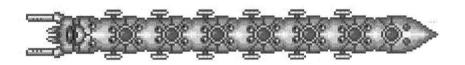

Players need to kill the Destroyer before the sun rise as it runs away if not defeated. The shared segments of the monster have a life of 80,000. ***Piercing weapons*** can be used effectively against the boss. The monster will try to trap you in its body. In such a situation you can use Grappling hooks. The monster can be summoned at night using a Mechanical Skull.

2. Skeletron Prime

Skeletron Prime in essence is the hard mode version of the Skeletron boss. The boss can be summoned at night using a Mechanical Skull.

The monster attacks using its appendages, and spinning head attack. The Skeletron has a long life so players may take a little while to defeat this enemy. It also needs to be killed before dawn or it uses an attack that will kill the player instantly.

You need to focus on damaging the Saw and Vice segments of Prime Skeletron. After damaging these segments, it becomes relatively easy to deal with the boss. Players can use *Gravitation potions* and *Hermes boots* to stay out of reach.

3. The Twins

The Twins can be considered as the hard mode version of Eye of Cthulhu. The Twins become much more dangerous in their second stage. The boss uses a charging attack that can cripple a player. It is difficult to dodge the attack. Players can use *Hermes Boots* to dodge the charging attack. The Twins can be summoned using a Mechanical Eye at night.

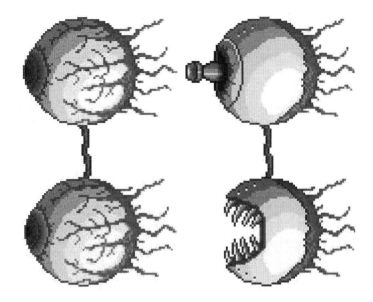

Chapter 4
TIPS, TIPS, STRATEGIES AND CHEATS TO SCORE HIGH IN THE GAME

1. GAME CHEATS AND STRATEGIES

STRATEGY FOR EATER OF WORLDS

Eater of Worlds can prove to be a difficult monster to deal with especially if you are not prepared. You can plan an effective strategy to defeat this monster. It is essential for you to build a big enclosed arena at a distance of few blocks from where you plan to summon the enemy.

This will help you keep smaller enemies from bothering you and the gap will permit you to get enough time to avoid the monster attacks. Moreover, if you have not obtained flail weapons you need to bring Shruikens (help you deal with consistent ranged damage) in a significant amount.

STRATEGY FOR PLAYING FLOATING ISLAND

It is significant for you to know that almost every randomly generated world has a floating island containing a chest filled with most unique loot items. Additionally, these islands are rich in Gold and Silver ores.

It can be a little difficult to locate a floating island as the altitude at which you can find a floating island has a direct correlation with the size of the world that you have created. Building a sky bridge can help you locate a floating island easily. In case you have built a small world, you can build a sky bridge at an altitude of 200 blocks above the sea level.

STRATEGY FOR SURVIVING IN THE UNDERGROUND JUNGLE

Almost every world has an underground jungle that is filled with creepy monsters and valuable items. You can find these biomes at the end of the world before the ocean. Walking straight in the same direction will lead you to one of these worlds.

If you have found Underground Jungle in the east direction, you will find the dungeon in the west. But it is advised to explore these jungles with strong armor to make sure that you are well equipped to handle the monsters showcased in these areas.

HARVESTING AND COLLECTING FALLEN STARS

An event occurs in the Terraria world at night during which stars fall from the sky. If you manage to collect ten of these fallen stars, it can increase your maximum Mana. Nonetheless, it can be a risky move in pitch darkness.

If you create a sky bridge (can be built by making a ladder from approximately 100 blocks and then lining dirt or stone in a straight line to complete the bridge) you will be able to create a safe landing place for stars.

You can then use *Necro armor* or *Hermes boots* to reach the height of your bridge and collect stars. Even though, zombies such as *Demon eye* and *Harpy* will still be able to spawn on your bridge you can use these equipments to deal effectively with these monsters.

GETTING INFINITE LIFE CRYSTALS AND CHEST ITEMS

In order to get infinite Chest crystals and Chest items out of the Chest, follow these steps,

1. Log on to Terraria.org and try downloading their dedicated program server.
2. You can use this server to start a world or create a new world (type local host into the IP address to join your own server).
3. You can then search for chests and life crystals then continue saving the game using the server command window before picking items.
4. Pick up chest items and life crystals as much as you can and then close the server window.
5. Now re open your server and join it. You will have your stored chest items and life crystals in your inventory items. If you go quickly back to the spot where you have found the stuff, you can still take the items. After picking the items close the server without saving and you will be able to pick up whatever you want, whenever you want.

DUPLICATING ITEMS

Save the progress of your game and make a backup of your saved game. Deposit the items you need in a chest. Then save your game and exit. Now go back into the game and take out the items that you want to duplicate and place it in your inventory. Wait for a few minutes and then close the game. Re open your game and you will have the duplicated item in your inventory and chest.

2. EFFECTIVE TIPS AND TRICKS TO SURVIVE IN THE TERRARIA WORLD

EFFECTIVE TIPS FOR COMABTING MONSTER S IN THE TERRARIA WORLD

1. Monsters spawn randomly in the Terraria world. It is suggested to place solid blocks when digging a vertical shaft to avoid monsters/enemies falling on the head on your character.

2. To hide from the Mother Slime, you can take refuge in holes. The monster would not be able to follow you into narrow holes.

3. Unless you have a Cobalt shield and Obsidian skull and Grappling Hook, do not try to explore the Underground World.

4. It is essential for you to know that you can shoot through platforms made of wood, so you can easily shoot monsters from the inside of your shelter.

5. If you manage to build a large platform above the surface (in the sky) or fight on the floating island, you would not have to worry about protecting your NPC's.

EFFECTIVE TIPS FOR MOVING AROUND IN THE TERRARIA WORLD

1. If you happen to fall from a height and you have Ivy Whip, Dual hook or Grappling Hook, firing it downwards can save you from getting fall damage. Additionally, Rocket Boots and Cloud in a bottle can also prevent you from receiving fall damage.

2. When working through Lava and water, placing blocks in the liquid permits you to build air pockets when trapped in tricky situations. You can use this technique to safely tunnel through lava.

3. When you are exploring Underground layers, digging artificial traps and air pockets will allow you to breathe, place torches and move easily between caves and lakes.

4. If you are significantly away from you spawn and you do not want to use the magic mirror to return quickly, you can use simply choose to leave the map and return to your spawn (the place where you started).

5. Carrying Piggy Bank in your inventory is a good idea since it works similar to chests (used for storing items).

EFFECTIVE TIPS FOR BUILDING IN THE TERRARIA WORLD

1. In order to prevent enemies from breaking in your house during Blood Moon, place a block on the inside or outside of your house. This will lock your door and prevent it from opening in the direction you placed the block.

   Furthermore, you can also use furniture to keep the door from opening. You can also consider building two doors at a significant distance from each other. This way, if you open the inside door in the outward direction it will block monsters from getting past the outer door and attack you.

2. It is also essential for you to know that an open door permits players to place sand on top of the open door. When you close the door, the sand tends to fall down thus permitting you to make traps.

3. You can also take refuge in holes to take a break from the game. Nonetheless, you need to beware of the Fire Imps, Dark Casters and Goblin Sorcerers.

4. Replacing a block (located two blocks away from water body) with a torch will help you lighten up an underwater area.

5. When you are building the back walls for huge buildings, you can use the Ivy Whip to position yourself in the centre of the room.

EFFECTIVE TIPS FOR MINING IN THE TERRARIA WORLD

1. If you need ores urgently, you can consider creating a new world and you will be able to find ores such as copper, iron and even Gold on the surface.

2. If you want to explore the underground world quickly (avoiding several other biomes), you can dig down straight through a Hell elevator (mine shaft that runs from the surface to the underground).

3. It is essential for you to drain as much water to the Hellworld as possible as it will become easier for you to fight the bone serpents and flying imps. Additionally, it will also decrease your chances of falling into the lava.

4. During your first few days in the Terraria world, it is significant for you to mine ores to craft armors and weapons to protect yourself against enemies such as Demon Eyes and Zombies.

5. It is also worthwhile to mention that some ores such as Adamantite, Cobalt and Mythril ore cannot be obtained before defeating the Wall of Flesh. However, if you break a significant number of Demon Altars you can obtain a good storage of these ores.

Chapter 5
FINAL WORD

To cut it short, from making weapons to digging deep underground to uncover hidden accessories, money and other valuables, from fighting tough enemies and monsters in a number of biomes, to gathering stone, ores, wood and other resources to build and defend your **Terraria** world, the game has something for everyone.

You will be provided with a limited number of resources in this game and you are required to utilize them in the best possible manner to defend yourself against the nocturnal monsters.

So what are you waiting for?! Grab your tools and get ready to face the challenge. Can you dig it?!

Maple Tree Books

If you want to get access to upcoming books on various topics, 'like' our Facebook page to be informed. We always offer the books for free for 5 days when they are first released. You can download them when they are free and benefit from them :)

Go to this website and enter your name and email to join our mailing list.

https://www.Facebook.com/mapletreebooks

And oh, dont forget to leave a review :)

Even if you did not benefit from this book at all we still want to hear from your feedback so we can improve in the future :)

Alternatively you can join our mailing list

http://www.MapleTreeBooks.com

You can join our Twitter page as well

https://Twitter.com/MapleTreeBooks1

Thanks for reading :)

We wish you success in this life and in the next.